LOOKING GOOD

LOOKING GOOD

CAROLE COATES

Shoestring Press

All rights reserved. No part of this work covered by the copyright
hereon may be reproduced or used in any form by any means –
graphic, electronic, or mechanical, including copying, recording, taping,
or information storage and retrieval systems – without written
permission of the publisher.

Typeset and printed by Q3 Print Project Management Ltd,
Loughborough, Leics
(01509) 213456

Published by Shoestring Press
19 Devonshire Avenue, Beeston, Nottingham, NG9 1BS
(0115) 925 1827
www.shoestringpress.co.uk

First published 2009
© Copyright: Carole Coates
The moral right of the author has been asserted.
ISBN: 987 1 904886 91 4

ACKNOWLEDGEMENTS

With acknowledgements to *Smith's Knoll, Other Poetry, Staple, Orbis, The Interpreter's House, Scintilla, The Frogmore Papers, Shadow Train, Obsessed with Pipework, Dream Catcher, Pennine Platform, Lancaster Literature Festival Competition Anthology 2005, The Vers Prize Anthology 2007, Hand Luggage Only*, edited Christopher Whitby 2007, *Speaking English*, edited Andy Croft 2007.

*For John and Charlotte
and for Criss who solves
all my computer problems*

CONTENTS

Bride Doll	1
Looking Good	3
Rabbit	4
Eat Me, Drink Me	5
Falling Down	6
High	7
A Winter's Tale	9
Baby	10
Exmouth Sunday	11
Red Shoes	12
Red Shoes	14
The Modification of Clouds	16
At the County Hospital	17
Mirror Woman	18
The Chocolate Machine on Pennsylvania Hill	19
Vacation	20
Vacation	21
This is your Proper Name	22
Through the Looking Glass	23
Eating God	24
Feast Day	25
Thermopylae	26
In the Morning	27
Home for Christmas	28
Distorted	29
Label	30
Twin	31
Strange Meeting	32
Fasting Saints	33
Girl	34
Vanishing Point	36
White Hair	37
Straw into Gold	39

II

Water Work	43
Clayton Branfoot and the Grimsby Chums	44
Woodbines	47

Umbratilis, Shade-loving	48
John in the Kitchen Reading	49
My Daughter does Stand-Up Comedy	50
Jacqueline	51
Writers' Rooms	52
Carole Coates of Catalina Island	53
Visitation	54
Beast's Palace	55
The only way it can be all right	56
Elegy	57
A Request for More Seriousness from the Spirit World	58

BRIDE DOLL

A new sort of doll, your grandmother says.

It's not a doll at all but
some Hittite queen shipped
via California.

It's one of those teenage dolls
(and you're nineteen).

Hollywood hair and
staring Aryan eyes
she'll goosestep towards you
with sleepwalking arms
held out, palms down
but not helpless, no – her fingers
taper to tiny needles.
Don't touch her.

*So much easier to dress
than dolls with stomachs,*
and your grandmother fetches
tulle by the yard, pearl beads, white ribbons…

Hard high cones for breasts –
almost spikes like the tops of railings.
Arms held out for embrace. No.
Click. Her eyes shut. Click. They open.

Plastic curve (infinitesimal)
to bum and thigh and then
pale giraffe legs, long and cool
as bluebell stalks, impossible,

and sharp little feet already tiptoed
for plastic stilettos which your grandmother
is now varnishing with silver.

She'll have roses and lilies
embroidered for her bouquet,
wear silk orange blossom flowers in her
unbelievable, appalling hair.

And here's the hand-made lace to cover
her nut-hard, impenetrable vagina.

LOOKING GOOD

She's looking good. It's May. There's an outburst of daisies
and her skirt falls round and down to her feet without touching
    her hips
so that she steps out shining and smiling. Cool white legs step
    out and step over.
She walks away, leaves it there, a denim chrysalis – shabby old
    thing.
There are white butterflies too which seem appropriate.
This morning the lecture is "Chaucer: *The Romaunt of the Rose*"
and she carries the heavy book up the hill in her brand-new
    jeans.

She reaches up to touch, if she can, the improbable pear-blossom.

RABBIT

All the windows are mirrors and cameras
filming her entry into the clear bright air
in the first May she's felt worthy of Spring.
The birds are singing for her. The sweet scrapings
from the high air are probably a lark's.
Star-like, she settles herself on the grass
midway between the myrtle and white camellia.

She's reading Keats's "Ode to a Nightingale"
when a white rabbit flops out of the rhododendron,
tastes the green scene, languorously.
It's going to be one of those whimsical days,
she thinks and addresses the rabbit.
Where are your gloves, white rabbit and where is your fan?
And where is the great dark hole we'll both fall in?

The eyes of the windows watch the silent rabbit
as the skinny girl writes in her diary
Lost six pounds this week. Saw a white rabbit.

EAT ME, DRINK ME

When I read *Alice* I was relieved
to find it had happened to her
although it was her fault for snacking
on food that was left about. Good children
never do such a thing because of Germs.

I was a good girl, but it only needed
the light to snap off at bedtime
and I was lost in the swelling, bloating
enormity of myself. Huge.
Ballooning, I bumped each corner
of the black muffle of night

until I dwindled, dwindled,
diminished, smaller,
smaller, tiny, smallest,
hardly there, a grain in the bedclothes,
a taste in the mouth, only that,
barely that...

I got to the light switch in time,
examined my hand, found a mirror –
I was back again. This was me.
Then I would read a book to forget about it.
Not *Alice* though, never *Alice*.
She was down underground with the worms and dead people.

FALLING DOWN

You choose *fino* not *amontillado*
because it is less gross.
You refuse an olive.

Your hungry eyes search
the bevelled glass.

You watch your elegant
articulation of bones.
You are eating yourself.

You refuse an olive.
Bruises flower blue on your legs.
You have almost perfected yourself.

It is always Lent and you are a Lenten lily.
You have given up the lunar flow of blood.
You are perfect as a snowflake travelling upwards
or the quarter moon, pale in the morning.

Yesterday, an apple entered you.
This morning, an orange segment.
You would sip air, have clouds for your food
while you feast on the good meat of yourself.

This sherry will down you.
It's as strong as the scent
of great brown wall-flowers.

This is fire-water, moon-shine.
It will down you and drown you.

You have almost perfected yourself
through a long murderous Lent.

You will fall. You are falling. You fall.

HIGH

Up on the roof again
and under my feet
a hundred people asleep
or thinking of sleep

Something will happen
up here in the not dark

The moon and the moonlit river
map out the night

I can feel it most up here

Down there huddled in a maze –
the cathedral's hunched shoulders
hazy scaffolding for the new store
hugger mugger, shrunken – the little city

Something will happen

Scent of powerful wallflowers
creeping up

and someone's singing to a muffled guitar
the words but not the tune of *Green Door*

Nearer, the silent X film outline of a bat

Still, so still

Watch me now
Shape-shifter
             Soul girl
bodiless almost

The stars will pay attention

I am invisible
against the chimneys

Something will happen
by an effort of my will.

A WINTER'S TALE – THE OPEN-AIR STUDENT PRODUCTION

She goes on a special Perdita diet – two green salads
and three raisins a day to give her energy.
She's made her costume in white voile with silver ribbons
and she's been to the florist and paid for the real flowers
that Perdita gives to the grown-ups, naming them one by one.

But it's chilly all day and a still, quiet cold in the evening
settles on rhododendron, terrace, querulous spectators
and the goose-pimpled arms of Perdita
whose flowers are thrown helter-skelter everywhere
when a hail-storm disrupts Act Three and scatters the audience.

Each grain of hail remains on the terrace.
Perdita holds some in her hand for a moment, studies them.
They are like small white currants. She begins to eat them.

BABY

Hunger is your baby.
You nurse her constantly.
You sling her at your breast

for the slow purposeful trudge,
but your breasts are flat,
she has nuzzled you so.

You show her your world –
meat, fruit and cheeses,
ten sorts of bread.

You're enticed by the deep
night-blue of poppy-seed
but you manage to turn away.

Dinner-time for Hunger –
you give her a rusk, five apple-seeds,
a thimble of skimmed milk.

Then you both sleep
cheek to cheek.
(You need so much sleep.)

EXMOUTH SUNDAY

He drops her radio on the beach –
grubby, unwashed, hopping with sand fleas.
He wants to hear *The House of the Rising Sun* –
This is the sort of thing he likes.
He fondles her without enthusiasm.

They're going to try the new craze – Ten Pin Bowling
which is giant skittles in a great shed
with coffee machines and shouting. Also food.
Absolutely not she says to a hot dog.
But when she tries to lift a ball, she can't.
She might as well have tried to shift Exmouth.
Frowning, he goes to find a child's ball.
He wins, of course. This is what he likes.

Silent on the train, they look away politely
to where the moon is interfering with the estuary.
That night she lies in bed and thinks of food.

RED SHOES

Your boyfriend won't guess
that Time is your lover –

who commands you to bed
before ten o'clock,
watches you all night
with his white blank eye;

who sends you at dawn,
naked to the weighing
and watches with you
for the quivering point;

who holds you at the wrist
with his lean brown finger,
then runs you round the block
over and over.

Two hundred minutes
between breakfast coffee
and lunchtime apple –
you count each moment.

Later, in the bar
with your puzzled boyfriend
you sip still water
and glance at your wrist.

That night in the club
you're too tired to dance
but you keep on dancing
through all the red noise.

You don't know you're wearing
time's red shoes.
These will keep you dancing.

RED SHOES

Weird that feet lose weight –
I could slide my foot now
into any prince's slipper
without cutting off a toe

(if I wanted to, that is).

All my old shoes
are binned, heels stubbed
out like fag ends.

But these new stilettos –
red as the tap shoes I once had.

Sally said (when I was taking notes
on <u>Rasselas</u>) *Why are you always
working? My mother knew a girl
who couldn't stop.*

But we'll go out tonight –
jostling at the mirror
with our black mascaras.
She'll try on my shoes.
The best bit is the tarting-up
together. We just laugh.

Who are we going to meet?
Not James again, who's reading Kerouac,
and – carless – wants to tramp the roads
with me. *What about baths?*

I said. He looked disgusted.
Worse was when I got off
with a lay preacher.

Getting ready for the Ball
is better than the Ball.
Any Cinderella knows that.

THE MODIFICATION OF CLOUDS

Last night the sky was grandiose above the estuary
like some enormous present. It almost made her cry.
So she's bought a book of clouds. She loves taxonomies
and she's walking backwards up the hill to see it better:
the cinema of the sky. Her boyfriend's gone to Land's End.
Cumulus is easy – vast chubby heaps of vapour – classic stuff.
There's a week-long birthday party. She won't go.
Stratus are the long lines underneath (in this case black).
Cumulo-stratus? Strato-cumulus? She can tick that off.
They lean from Exmouth to the Haldon Hills.
Cider, pasties, beer, crisps, fruit cake, marzipan.
But when she looks again the sky's escaped
and there are rags of air flapping her face.
The cloud has ruined itself, cancelled its form,
collapsed into a black sheet, spreading northwards.

She sits the cloud-burst out under a tree.
It's probably raining harder in Land's End.
An image returns, re-forms, asserts itself –
Her grandmother told her of an operation
where yellow slabs of fat spilled from the body.
Just look at that, the surgeon said.

Walking downhill under a clearer sky
she sees the high clouds, like iced feathers.
They are called alto-cirrus. They are out of it all.

AT THE COUNTY HOSPITAL

They haven't told her why and she doesn't really care
that her eggs have stopped blobbing every month.
In her head she's still somewhere else
in the self-induced trance of being miles away
when all those men put their hands inside her.

She wonders if they've dried up at the source –
or there's a build-up somewhere, a brimming dam of marshy
blood?

She doesn't ask, but the chief doctor with the biggest hands
smiles towards her, bends down over her.
He's had a good look round and he's found nothing wrong.
But maybe she's *just a teeny bit too thin?*
Doctor's orders – a box of Cadbury's Milk Tray.
And put your feet up too – some chocs, an Agatha Christie....

She smiles and nods – she has the manners of obedience.
Her mother always said she was too good to live.

MIRROR WOMAN

If you eat butter
you know what will happen.

The glass bulges and thickens.
The mirror woman comes.

She is your unspeakable relative.
How long will she stay?

She is the bag lady
who knows your secret
and shouts it in the street.

She is more than pear-shaped –
a full sack swelling downwards.

She is thick as earth,
sullen as water.

She is the slag heap
that shifts on the mountain

and will find its level
in a curve of gravity,
a flesh waterfall.

She is the mud surge
which will bury you.
You know what to do.

THE CHOCOLATE MACHINE ON PENNSYLVANIA HILL

Rain is gagging the estuary.
It's soaked every bush on Pennsylvania,
consumed the shrubberies in a mess of cloud.

Midnight and only snails should be out
but something famished is coming down the hill
in sneakers and cagoule. (She's calculating purges,
fasts, hard exercise to compensate for this.)

There's someone there who scares her, speaks her name –
her Mediaeval tutor, white moustache wet through.
Her name for him is *Gawaine*. She answers him,
tells him why she's there. *But why on earth.......?*

 But now she's caught the whisky on his breath,
and turns away disgusted. Walking back,
she flings the chocolate in the shrubberies.

She'll get up earlier, work harder, longer,
walk further, maybe buy a skipping rope.
She'll pay anyway. She's looking forward to it.

VACATION

She must be looking good – her dad's just walked past her.
He's come to collect her, searching for his daughter.

Her mother accuses her of being tubercular
(embarrassing though when she screams at the sight of her)

while her gran, the old nurse, shakes her head very slowly
and takes her out shopping at Sainsbury's.

She could rise in the air, touch the Guinness hoarding.
She could float away up The Western Avenue.

She must tell her grandmother but she can't catch up with her.
She's walking so briskly and her stick taps inexorably.

VACATION

My mother can't bear to watch me dying
(she says). She sits in the Public Library

and pretends to read. So now
I've become my grandmother's child.

This is temporary. We collaborate
on salads, negotiate meat, weigh apples.

She feeds me careful cubes of chicken.
I'm her very good tabby cat

(for the time being). But my mother
cooks chips in a seething golden haze,

makes toffee at midnight
with a dark reek of sugar,

and, out for lunch the other day,
while I ate three tenths of a salad,

she gorged on Knickerbocker Glory.
No protein. No vitamins. I told her that.

She laughed and ordered a Drambuie.
Now she's eating bread and marmalade

with huge glaring bites. There's something
wild about her. Feral? Yes, she's feral.

THIS IS YOUR PROPER NAME

I shall call you Starving –
all other names
are candy, marshmallow.

Starving, you're not a witch,
not a bully man –
no one to blame.

You're not too little,
not a vanishing.
You're too much.

Starving, you're not a desert place.
You're an ocean
where people walk

learn to breathe water
move through dark matter.
More come every day.

THROUGH THE LOOKING GLASS

Alice didn't care what she was wearing
but I do – dragged through the revolving door

of the looking glass in my trodden-down slippers
and the cold sore red on my lip and no mascara,

me, in my old brown coat with the torn collar –
into a brand-new place. Think of Versailles

but more glittering, refurbished, each mirror
polished to wincing. Even the floor is glass

and on the ceiling, morbid crystal growths
of chandeliers. And me, like a chimney sweep

among the mirrors. Now the oboes sound
and a line of girls advances in white satin

with nodding ostrich feathers in their hair.
This one – tiny, as pale as ivory,

intricately turning on the mirrored floor
like a clockwork dancer on a music box.

But they are all clockwork dancers
with elegant painted eyes. I want to shout

You're just a pack of dolls, but I'm stuck
in the tired situation of my body –

and they are all around me, turning
and staring, staring with elegant painted eyes.

EATING GOD

She's never wanted to talk to God
or priests or any other old man
but there's something wrong in her head
which aspirin doesn't help, or doctors.
She goes back to her grandmother's religion.

Fellatio she thinks as she opens her mouth
for the host – but it's carbohydrate,
sticks to the roof of her mouth
like a dry sacred rice cake.

It's blasphemy to poke it with a finger
or even use her teeth to scrape it off
so she kneels with her head bent
gagging and licking the host
with a tongue parched as a feather.

Later she receives confession.
But the old priest behind the curtain
says in a puzzled Irish voice
You're only young – you should enjoy yourself.

FEAST DAY

This is your meal – formal as the levée
of a royal personage, some pale Infanta
decked out for Corpus Christi.

For how but in custom and in ceremony
could you expose your body
to this extreme event?

Try a pale kidney, naked from the grill
or the small moist heart of a lamb chop
or the white breast of a tiny bird.

You've renounced the treason of vegetables
since butter, like a dagger,
was concealed in the dish.

Once you sliced the globe of an egg
and its yellow eye stared at you.
You're like a funeral or a coronation.

Perform your stately and exiguous feeding.
People might even pay to watch you eat –
some would give anything to see it.

THERMOPYLAE

How many months since those raucous days
when the Beatles played the Odeon
and there was that great party in Kilmorie
(twist, shout, hands flung up to the ceiling)?
She ate too much and was chased round the building
by a tall young man called Sam. *You're missing your chance,*
he yelled, *with one of the lords of life.*
She drank too much and fell off her bike later
and slept on someone else's floor under an umbrella.
It seemed to be happiness – she remembers it –
but she must be mistaken. In those days she was fat.

Now she wants to get out of the Students' Union
where The Small Faces are playing
in a bored trance, their sleek profiles averted.
She's twenty and she's stopped being young.

She prefers to be out on the boundary road
in the dark with spurts of rain and wind.
In this austere and solitary walking
there's an ecstasy – like early flying
or holding the pass among the barren mountains –
stoic, against all odds, wondering
is this the end or is it the beginning?

IN THE MORNING

Lie down a stone and rise up a loaf –
that's what her grandmother always says
but today she is entirely stone –
stone and weighed with stone, pressed down by stone.

Her hand moves, slow as glaciers, to her watch.
It's like being dead and knowing about it.
Gravity is different now she's dead
and thoughts harden to a lead drop.

Much later she stalks the corridor
then lies in the bath, watching her grey knees.
Can she cry even? Yes, she can cry.
It's being dead and knowing everything about it.

HOME FOR CHRISTMAS

The only thing you like is the tree
because it is inedible. You plunge
your face into its branches, inhale
cold forests, northern lights, snow...

but your traitor mother
heaps food all round you –
pork pies, mince pies, sausage rolls...
Eat this. Try another.

You take the old dog
for a walk it doesn't want
round and round the park
empty on the hill

in a cartoon of suburbs,
pop-up cut-outs from a children's book.
All the quiet streets – dolls-house facades,
tinselled with lit bulbs behind them.

Trudge back towards Christmas dinner
where your traitor Vichy body
will collude with the enemy.
Punish her for that.

Shave her head. Starve her.

DISTORTED

Starving makes you stupid.
You didn't know it then.
You could re-write history
from this insight.

That old dear, Cleopatra, for example.
Would she have left Antony treading water
at Actium if her brain hadn't narrowed
as well as her waistline?

And as for your Thermopylae –
I've been there recently
on a kind October day with leaves like asters.
I walked your arduous path so easily.

But you remember the austere and solitary walking,
rock walls dripping wet, a wind from the sea.

At your Thermopylae there were no Persians.
No Spartans at your side.
No one will say
I fought with you at the Hot Gates.

No one was there but you
and you were starving
stumbling up the rocky path
in an exultation
both stupid and ecstatic.

I remember it.

LABEL

That was the year they made her ordinary.
Other things happened. Someone shouted Judas.
A long war started. A ball game was won.

An ordinary Sunday: Nescafé, Ryvita,
sunlight on the Observer Magazine –
its list of all the fun decade's diseases.

They'd given her a strange name
and brain doctors were hard at work
composing banal narratives for her

and all the thousands like her.
Ordinary. She ran into the hall
where the long mirror gleamed.

Who was this woman?
Pilgrim? Lone flyer? No.
The landscape in her head spilled out –

a hawk pacing the wind
above the rock-strewn pass, the austere air,
the long view down the valleys –

smudged now, losing its identity
as a patch of bright weather
is blotted out by black Atlantic rain.

This is a discarded photograph
of a thin girl. There are many like her.
It is quite an ordinary thing.

TWIN

One child has a twin
locked in her body.
While she grows, it remains
unformed, embedded –
a feather or two of bone
seeded in the flesh,
a wisp of hair, a shadow
of vertebrae, curving nowhere,
even a tooth in the uterus –
her rag and bone sister
who calls out in dreams.

My own twin
is less diffused –
a clenched fist of a ghost
made flesh in my flesh
in a cold indwelling
lasting decades. And noisy.
Even now, among leached bones,
loosening flesh, she keeps on.
(I know her eyes are hard
and blue and round as millstones.)
She keeps on. *Starve,* she says,
Starve. You fool.

STRANGE MEETING

If we could meet, it should be in
a place of glass – plant-house,
aquarium – in some botanic park.
There would be rain above us
gliding round the curving panes;
a noise of pipes, a dripping hose,
the tiny sounds of fish rising in cisterns
to mouth the exotic air.

There will be palms, tree-ferns, banana leaves,
lilies and orchids – this one oddly called *Dracula Bella*,
and here you are under the stag's horn ferns
watching an axolotl in its tank
retain its *aquatic newt-like larval form*.
Poor thing – it's motionless as a gilled stone.

I want to warn you of the troubles coming
– the consequences. But I stop
shocked, maybe, by your emaciation
or something else.
She's free, I think, then wonder what I mean.
You turn your face
(my face and not my face)
and say to the decaying air
I never want to look like her,
then turn again back to the axolotl,
that stalled and pensive beast which never
will become a salamander.

The Axolotl is a large Mexican salamander noted for remaining in its immature aquatic larval form as a sexually mature adult and not undergoing metamorphosis into a terrestrial form.

FASTING SAINTS

Fina was a girl who died for God
Sancta Fina, Beata Fina.
She lay on a board, refused all food.
Thus we can understand

how easy it is to be a saint.
And look at the support she had –
as much as Bobby Sands.
And look at her reward.

Every little slug and worm,
spider, earwig, louse and flea
transformed to roses in her bed.
She must have been good

with angels ringing bells
and all those miracles,
the greatest of these –
her thick golden hair

her rosy round head,
which was after death removed
for a bust-reliquary
with hair of pure gold.

(But what grand narrative did I employ
forty years back to think my lice were roses?)

Saint Fina, protector of the town of San Gemignano, died in 1253, and is commemorated by a Renaissance chapel in the Collegiate church there.

GIRL

You're three feet high – with wings.
Some-one silver-pencilled you there
where the syringa will, one day,
bud blank-white as your dress.

Soon the old man next door
will buy you, but not your sister,
an ice-cream, and you'll begin
to learn the power of wings.

Much later, you'll wear
wings in white on black
as if by Mary Quant.
But you're not confident.

A young man will bring
a corsage of orchids –
curved scrapes of wax
freckled with dried blood.

Next, wings blue-green as oil in the rain.
You'll not be sure of the man with blonde hair
who brings you from Glastonbury
the riff from his guitar.

Your wings are red, thatchered with power.
You'll get what you want, then change your mind.
Your booty will include garnets, hearts, gardenias,
black pearls, a small car like a plum.

But then comes Requisition afternoon.
Your wings will be recalled –
detached, not painlessly –
removed, not without sound

and you'll be left in the dry day
wondering if you ever learnt to fly
or was it silver paper, cardboard, a high wind?

Your daughter will find
a photo of a girl,
three feet high, with wings.

VANISHING POINT

She skulked on the top landing
eavesdropping and being invisible.
She envied spiders, watched beetles
for tips; spied on houseflies
and all overlooked creatures.
She avoided games; refused cake;
at parties, sat in a corner reading;
would erase herself in a book –
they were never long enough.
She desired her shadow's distance,
that private way it had.
She peeled her flesh, rasher by rasher;
wept minerals to leech her bones;
shaved her head; was a reed, etiolated,
but found she had gained attention
rather than vanishment.
Men, especially, would survey her.
Later, she disgorged children;
followed her shadow about;
did the chores, all in plain sight
until on her fiftieth birthday
she was given the perfect present.

She's quite dissolved, now, into the mise-en-scène.
Eavesdropping at parties, who observes her?
All she had to do was wait.

WHITE HAIR

Once upon a time, we were out walking
one fine May morning,
Catherine and me in the Coulston Road
in denims and long, long hair.

Two young men were out walking,
strolling behind us
and started the old routine,
Hey blondie, hey gorgeous!
What about a kiss then?

and we turned round and smiled
our hearts full of malice
but mildly saying
Didn't that give you a fright, then?

Sorry, ma'am, sorry ma'am,
the young men apologised,
horrified, horrified,
for we were as old as their mothers.

So I cut off my hair
out of pity for poor young men.

But now it's gone white
I will grow it and grow it
and go walking in Springtime
in denims and long, long hair.

And all the young men shall be safe:

now, there are men, I'm told,
who find white hair sexy.
I've never met one
but he would be thumb-sucking and fattish
with a heart full of malice.
Don't trust him.

STRAW INTO GOLD

She's locked in the kitchen looking at the straw
while Daddy Grizzly with his friendly hug
and the children with their sharp fox eyes

and the new baby with the crocodile jaw
(and the fat dog and the fat cat and Hammy the hamster)
are hanging up their stockings at the mantelpiece –

flaccid and empty, waiting to be filled,
mouths gaping in a listless O
and she's in the kitchen looking at the straw

which is bigger than a haystack, bigger than a house.
Lucky she's got her own O, empty as Heaven,
a pure zero somewhere on her person.

She begins to nibble, then chews like a goat
thoroughly, thoroughly, chomps like a horse.
She's mouth and teeth and gaping throat,

oesphagus, peristalsis, great gut –
gulps it down. Wads of straw, dry husks,
ten fields of dry grass, wilderness fodder.

She gulps it down in a dreary frenzy,
and rolls on the floor, stuffed with straw,
bigger than a haystack, bigger than a house.

Bang. Bang. They bang on the door –
Big Daddy Grizzly, fox-eyed children
and the new baby with the crocodile jaw.

Give us our gold now, woman.
Give us the gold we promised you.
Give us our impossible gold.

II

WATER WORK

This was the best that Henrietta Scott
could manage. She hauled water from
the pump in Drury Lane up five flights
to her room in the waterless house. She clanked buckets
to scrub Covent Garden floors – straw, shit, mud,
gobbets of phlegm, cabbage leaves, egg, the bloodstains of beetroot –
all excised, scoured and sent in filthy water
through gullies, drains and gutters
and gothic passages of sewers down
to the ponderous important river. She swilled out privies,
carted water uphill, upstairs; scrubbed attics;
washed out cellars when the sewers flooded.

She was my great great grandmother.
Her daughters became washerwomen.
These women who carried water from pumps and wells
had raw chapped fists, back ache, throbbing chilblains,
prolapses, arthritic knees, varicose veins, T.B.
Their bodies are intimately connected with mine.

                                            Let water remember.
Let it leap from the tap crying *your mother did this
and your grandmothers*. Water, remember them all.
Henrietta Scott. Water, remember her
and Sara, her daughter, and her sister Rose.
Remember them all hauling water when water was rigid,
holding tight in winter, when gritty drippings
hardened to ice and windows thickened and bulged with it.

Let water remember them.

CLAYTON BRANFOOT AND THE GRIMSBY CHUMS

1. The Film

There's one fixed camera staked out in a field
while all the Grimsby Chums are marching past:
boys mainly, looking seriously ahead,
every cap pulled hard over the eyes.
Some of them seem to be wearing false moustaches.

I could pretend I know their names
or try to guess what they might say
but all I see in this old film
is a strange forfeiture of children
enticed away by some malign Pied Piper.

Great lads, big boys, teenagers, sweaty kids –
they march to music I can't hear.
I watch them training with their Lee-Enfields;
Company Drill, Entrenching, Charging Trenches.
They are a thousand ignorant dead faces.

2. Back Home

"You don't know it's a ghost until long after" –
I read this somewhere and now I wonder
about the Grimsby folk, left behind, making do:
fish dock empty, lighthouse darkened, terraces gone quiet.

Did they feel exposed under limitless grey sky
with the muddy flatlands stretching behind them?
The North Sea was also the German Ocean
and the Humber River was chained like a dog.

Further north, a destroyer bombarded Scarborough:
a man fell off his bike, restaurants were deserted,
The Grand Hotel was seriously incommoded –
this was, everyone agreed, a German atrocity.

So it was wonderful to go to The Tivoli
to see their boys, their own Tenth Battalion.
Seventeen rare moments of opportunity
to pick out and call after son or sweetheart.

Two days before, Kitchener's New Army
had risen at command and walked towards the guns
at a steady pace so the gunners got their range.
Generals thought the new men would turn tail.

News of the Somme took a week or more to travel.
What did they say, those women, when they thought of the film?
Men already dead marching in Lincolnshire
and they had cheered them on thinking them alive.
You don't know it's a ghost until long afterwards.

3. The Unofficial Grave

Twenty young men swagger –
arm in arm, legs straddled
helmets tipped anyhow
teeth intact and grinning
bones akimbo.

Mates buried by their mates –
never a formal do.
They could be off to the pub
a raucous phalanx
strutting into the dark.

All in a line –
even the odd leg
retrieved, put in place.
Chums of course
best left together.

Were they killed
by friendly fire?
A British gun
was firing short
that day.

4. The End of the Film.

The film proceeds with boxing, field kitchen and NCOs –
the sergeants joke and jostle for the camera.
Then officers with swagger sticks
and I know him at once.
He laughs, throwing his whole body back
then turns towards me with my mother's smile.
Not young, not tall, not thin, not like a soldier –
Clayton Branfoot, my grandfather's brother.
I know his dark ironic look.
"I'm here," he's saying, "but not entirely.
I have my own ideas about all this."
His photo shows a faded cardboard soldier,
but the difference between a still and moving picture!
Then low mist among trees, cold breath of the fields,
and a rider cantering off with a brisk wave.
I rewind, watch for him again.

A local film record of The Tenth Battalion, The Lincolnshire Regiment (the Grimsby Chums) training at Brocklesby, Lincolnshire in 1915, was specially taken for the Tivoli Cinema, Grimsby and first screened there on 4th July 1916, three days after the destruction of half the battalion on the first day of the Battle of the Somme.

The remains of twenty British soldiers were discovered at Point du Jour near Arras in 2001. Archaeologists unearthed the corpses, which were lying arm in arm. The men who were killed on 9th April 1917 were from The Tenth Battalion, The Lincolnshire Regiment.

Second Lieutenant C. Branfoot died Saturday, 25th August, 1917.

WOODBINES

Light up. I want to sniff
that first sharp instant
of a cigarette. Remind me of him.

So, wear a donkey jacket
lettered at the back and in the pocket
store a white impeccable handkerchief.

Could you drive a low-loader,
double-declutch the Pennines,
deliver the *golf balls* to Fylingdales

and keep your foot off the brakes,
steady your lorry on ice
on the narrow black road to Scotland?

Can you say – without a twist
of irony – *We are British working men
and together we can stand against all this?*

Oh, you are not like him, no.
There are no men like him now.

UMBRATILIS, SHADE-LOVING

It means you reading in the chestnut woods
or in the loggia listening to the bees
and the dry clatter of belled sheep returning.

The Romans were so strong on civic virtues
they couldn't comprehend unworldliness,
consigning it to *umbra,* shadow, shade...

A man who loves the shadows cast by leaves:
so this is your real home, Umbratilis –
this tributary, this valley,

this Umbrian farmhouse where a hidden bird
cheeps all day in the stonework.
The chestnut hills lean on the day's back

as calm as windless air, but not the air
beneath the trees, which is complicated
and clusters into shadowy meditations

which maybe you can understand.
But now you're reading Vergil on bee-keeping
who recommends the shade of wild trees.

JOHN IN THE KITCHEN, READING

Expert in words, food and whistling
and all the vocabulary of kitchen:

the sturdy epic of casseroles,
epigrams of peppers and spices;

you know the long poem of the Welsh dresser
which is full of adjectives – too many I would say.

On the window sill, a vernacular of milk jugs
and on the marble top, whole dialects of cheeses.

Now, the window tilts morning and clouds
are verbs, too irregular to memorise.

Other syntaxes persist in woks and saucepans
but the mirror conforms to the grammar of sunlight

and there's the noun of you – singular you –
centre page, as complete as a sonnet.

MY DAUGHTER DOES STAND-UP COMEDY

We're watching Canada geese square up to the swans
and a moorhen darting for cover
with no chance at all of the stale sliced bread.

That reminds me, she says and gives me a flyer,
an ad (glossy, six colours) for her latest gig
in King's Cross (Pentonville Road).

Centre front – a girl's face, Nordic blonde –
wings ringed with flame, like the cherubim
and what might be head-phones or maybe a halo.

She's no angel though, squinty and sulking
with collagen lips. No siren either.
She couldn't be arsed with all that.

Her wings are chrome-blue. They would clack
like Venetian blinds if she flew,
a bodiless super-model, over the Avon.

Is this supposed to be you? She raises her eyes to the clouds
which are heavy and dull as Canada geese.
You can't come though. Don't even think of coming.

JACQUELINE

On the small screen in the stiff front room
(in the faraway black and white Sixties)

her long bright hair showed pale as ash
but still flowed down like willow trails.

She had the look of a hawk, honed and intent.

As usual, she'd got dressed in a high wind,
bare legs, skirts flaring, something blown away.

She didn't care. She was the woman
with the long bright hair who played the cello

and embarrassed the men I knew
with her spraddled legs.

She sprawled back, eyes shut, without apology
discovering the music that she pulled
from the grave cello between her bony knees.

Good God, she's masturbating, one man said.

I said,
she's not looking at you,
she's not doing this for you.

               then heard her tear
the colours from the shapes
and set them hurtling free.

WRITERS' ROOMS

That snug or spacious attic
or sunny first floor front with leafy windows:
suspect them all, particularly their details –
kids' photographs; collections of Italian fans
or Christmas snow-globes; stones from Chesil Beach;
those drifts of well-loved books; the box of diaries
freighted with anecdote and reminiscence.

Look for zero ground,
white space, some sky room
with giddy horizontals,
an Arctic emptiness.

At least a room without a view or mirror
and let there be a smell of icy grass.

In the meantime, make do with a steel table
in the café at the swimming baths.
The steamed-up window and the wall of noise
will help. Or the plastic shelf,
just wiped over, at the coffee bar
in Oxford's covered market.
Try the library in Penrhydeudraeth,
its frosted window and high stone wall.
Or the last shelter on the promenade
where Brighton ebbs away to the marina.

They'll do at a pinch. They'll do for the time being.

CAROLE COATES OF CATALINA ISLAND

Woman with my name, American me,
you chose one of the lives I never
managed – any more than I attained
that long-limbed Aryan look. Golden hair
loose; your white dress streaked
and splashed by the Pacific, sun
making a fretted pattern through your hat,
you search for pottery from Gatsby days:
blue-patterned cups for tea in Avalon
and five-tiered cake-stands or the dinner set
left on the beach when everyone got drunk
in 1928. I would have liked a china shop
on Catalina Island.

                        Do you, self-googling,
wonder about me? Do I live one of the lives
you might have tried? Do you, among the glowing
orange groves, imagine writing rainy poetry
on this cool island? As I like pottery
(especially your art deco greens and blues)
do you write secret poems? When you
dive in the ocean, fighting its salt thickness,
do you look up to see the sunlit surface
gleam like stained glass? When you turn toward California
do you wonder how to hold that instant
of blossoming skeins of light along the shore?

VISITATION

The lilies have come, uninvited, into my house.
A couple recline on the chaise-longue, more
obscure the doors, crowd the stairs, some
have strewn themselves on my bed where
they bleach the counterpane with their fierce white.

My blue cushions with the fish pattern, the tulip curtains –
all losing their identity.

African Blues or Peruvian Orange Kings – those are
almost domestic, but these albino beasts
are beyond all proportion and, if I touch one,
it will scald my hand with the cold flame
of ice and phosphorus.

Harsh erotic lily-stink and drifts
of dangerous pollen grip my breath,
grasp my lungs, so that my voice is high
as a child's as I go from one to another
asking them to leave.

                    But it's like the moon,
visiting: not to be looked at or spoken to.

There's something that I recognise
in this huge, this overpowering whiteness,
but I'm wrong probably, as silly as waving
at a post in a green sea, or a queer-shaped rock
at the other side of the glacier.

These pale presences increase, increase –
an infinitely slow explosion of white lily.

BEAST'S PALACE

Look at his gifts –
parterres, a garden,
mountains like clouds

and this house
full of music
silver as air.

He comes near
sometimes – we know
by a catch of the breath

a mist on the eye
but most of our time
he stays away.

(We are blessed
in our jailor
the sorrowful Beast.)

When will he come
with his ambulance
and his black clothes?

*The only way it can be all right
is if we wake up forgetting everything
we have to forget everything*

This is what the little girl said
when her appalling parents went away
but could not also take their terrible presence.

We should try to give her what she wants.
Let her, let us, wake each morning
entirely new and uncorrupted.

The sunlight will amaze us or the rain
and the extraordinary coming on of night.
Clocks and timers will be children's toys.

The consequences of our acts will be forgotten.
Time will persist, but we can pardon Time.
This is the only way we can be happy.

ELEGY

Comrades you said. You said *brothers and sisters*.
These are words from the country that left us;
the island thrust down again into the sea;
a dead language now from a place dismantled,
folded up, packed and put out of reach
by goblins – well, what else can you call them?

Remember the trees, how they turned into fingers,
fat fingers with rings on? And the sky, how it fell
and became soft furnishings? We expected the loss
of childhood and love, but not this extinction...
and the words blown about diminished streets
or pulped for catalogues and magazines.

You spoke those words distinctly.
Brothers and sisters you said. *Comrades.*

A REQUEST FOR MORE SERIOUSNESS FROM THE SPIRIT WORLD

Brown river unrolling through the wet town –
I pause to watch the antics of a trolley,
loosed from the supermarket, snagged on a rock
and jerked about by rushing waters.
Didn't Wordsworth have a phrase for this?
*Blank misgivings of a creature
moving about in worlds not realised.*
That's you, I say to the trolley, *and it's me.*

What a great press the spirit world has had –
quite undeserved these days.
We don't expect an angel, no six-winged
being with a starlit face, but something more
than séances in disused cinemas. *Is there a Lizzie present?*
I've got her granny here. She says she's fine.

A gull swoops down to the trolley, veers away.
I could do better, I say to the wet air.
*From the black dot of my umbrella
by the lean brown-rushing river,
I'd rise from rainy Kendal
and fly through grey vapour
to Helvellyn's storm clouds
to talk with my mother.*

She'd like that after years of being dead.
But you don't get a choice with these sort of phenomena,
have to do with the trivial: spoon-bending, apports,
the hiding of tea-strainers, moving of pencils and walnuts
to inappropriate places, urgent fusillades of pointless knockings.
Three ducks are paddling for the trolley. They'll be disappointed.